THE LIFE AND TIMES OF

FRANK SINATRA

Esme Hawes

CHELSEA HOUSE PUBLISHERS
Philadelphia

First published in traditional hardback edition

Printed in Hong Kong

Unit 13–17, Avonbridge Trading Estate, Atlantic Road
Avonmouth, Bristol, England BS11 9QD

Illustrations courtesy of Hulton Deutsch Collection; London Features International; Mirror Syndication International; Peter Newark's American Pictures

Library of Congress Cataloging-in-Publication Data
Hawes, Esme.
The life and times of Frank Sinatra / by Esme Hawes.
p. cm.
Originally published: Avonmouth, Bristol : Parragon Book Service, 1996.
Summary: Surveys the career, hit records, films and personal life of the popular singer and actor.
ISBN 0-7910-4639-7 (hc)
1. Sinatra, Frank, 1915- —Juvenile literature. 2. Singers—United States—Biography—Juvenile literature. [1. Sinatra, Frank, 1915- 2. Entertainers.] I. Title.
ML3930.S58H39 1997
782.42164'092—dc21
[B] 97-25212
CIP
AC MN

CONTENTS

The Voice

HOBOKEN YEARS

In 1914 Hoboken, New Jersey, was a small city with seventy thousand inhabitants. Once a seaside resort for wealthy New Yorkers, it had become an industrial wasteland, flooded by wave upon wave of refugee immigrants to the New World. First to arrive—and therefore highest on the social ladder—were the Germans, then the Irish, and finally the Italians. Among the Italians, the northerners considered themselves vastly superior to those from the south—the Sicilians were deemed the lowest in the pecking order. One of the northern Italians was a pretty nineteen-year-old named Dolly Garavante. When she started dating a twenty-year-old boxer named Anthony Martin (Marty) Sinatra, her parents were horrified. He was tattooed, illiterate, asthmatic, unsuccessful as a boxer—and he was Sicilian. Despite her parents' objections, however, Dolly took Marty to the Jersey City registry office on Valentine's Day 1914, and, without further ado, married him.

The young couple was better off than many of their new neighbors since they could at least speak English. Dolly's blonde hair and blue eyes enabled her to pass herself off as an Irishwoman, which she frequently did, calling herself Mrs. O'Brien. Marty hung around the pool tables and remained a quiet, background figure in her life. Whenever Irish politicians needed Italian votes, they came to the woman with the rough language and the enormous personality and her loud, raucous laugh could be heard all over town. On December 12, 1915, Dolly gave birth to a thirteen-and-a-half-pound boy, who was dragged out with forceps that punctured an eardrum, tore an ear, and gouged his face and neck. The birth was so traumatic that Dolly was never able to have another child, so she became fiercely determined to make the most of this one. She also took up midwifery.

Ambitious for her new son, Dolly defied tradition and picked an Irishman instead of an Italian to be his godfather. Dolly was still too ill after the birth to attend the christening and, when the godfather—Frank Garrick, a newspaper manager—was asked for the name, he absentmindedly gave the priest his own name rather than the one chosen for the new baby, Anthony Martin like his father. The priest duly christened the new baby "Francis." When she was told, Dolly thought the accident was a good omen. The boy remained Francis Albert Sinatra.

On April 2, 1917, President Woodrow Wilson declared war against Germany and made Hoboken a principal embarkation port for U.S. troops. The Germans who had run the town for years were either rounded up and shipped to Ellis Island or fled. The Irish suddenly found themselves in charge and moved into the empty German areas of the city, while the Italians flooded into the former Irish areas, and their votes became even more important. Dolly Sinatra was called to the mayor's office, where she was given the job of official interpreter to the local court in return for telling the Italians which way to vote in elections. Despite her new and influential position, her own family was constantly in trouble with the law and her youngest brother, Babe, was sent to jail for ten years for his involvement in a murder during an armed robbery.

Once Dolly had firmly established herself as someone who could be guaranteed to deliver the votes, she began to make demands on the local council. In 1927, although there were no vacancies in the fire department, she saw to it that

Marty became a fire officer with an annual salary of $2000. Dolly immediately moved the family to a splendid three-bedroom apartment just outside Little Italy.

Now twelve years old, Frankie, already self-conscious about his facial scars, had become extremely thin and spindly following a recent appendectomy. His mother, who firmly believed that money solved all problems, dressed him up in expensive clothes, which only made him feel ridiculous. He was the only child in the neighborhood to have his own bedroom, and when he and his friends started a baseball team, Dolly bought every boy a flashy outfit, thereby ensuring that her son was made captain.

As the local midwife, one of her more lucrative sidelines was performing abortions. Everyone in the local community relied on Dolly to save their daughters from disgrace, though they then snubbed her socially because of her profession. Dolly soon found herself with a steady business, charging $25 to $50 for the treatment, and the Sinatra house, which was one of the few in the area with some spare cash, was always the scene of parties and noise.

In 1931 Frank started high school and dashed his mother's high hopes for his academic career by being expelled for "general rowdiness" after forty-seven days. Dolly was furious but had to accept it—he simply did not want to stay in school. She told him to find himself a job, but Frank didn't know how. Dolly called his godfather and asked him to give Frank a job at the newspaper. Nobody in their right mind crossed Dolly Sinatra, so Frank was immediately taken on as a delivery boy.

Dolly, however, had grander ideas. Within a few weeks she heard that one of the sports writers had been killed in a car crash. She immediately told her son to go and get the dead man's job. Frank took his mother's advice literally. The next morning he went into the newspaper office, sat down at the dead man's desk, and started sharpening pencils. When the outraged editor learned that Garrick had not given the boy the job, he demanded that Frank be dismissed on the spot. Frank was furious, blaming everything on his godfather, but there was little that Frank Garrick could do. Dolly never spoke to Garrick again, and it was fifty years before Frank and his godfather were reconciled. "My son is like me," Dolly used to say. "You cross him and he never forgets."

By 1932 Dolly was wealthy enough to move again—this time to a four-story house with dazzling modern decor. She had a baby grand piano, draped with a Spanish shawl, and a gilded birdbath decorated with golden cherubs holding red plastic roses. She continued to perform abortions in the basement, however. One went badly wrong and Dolly was arrested and put on probation for five years. This did not stop her, however, and neither did subsequent arrests, as she knew her political influence would keep her out of jail. Her Irish neighbors, though, were profoundly shocked and ostracized both her and her son, who felt the hurt deeply.

On Saturday nights Marty would go downtown to drink with the guys and Dolly would go out with her friend Rose. The two women would hit every political meeting in town, drink beer, and sing "When Irish Eyes Are Smiling." Frank hung around with local musicians and sang at school dances, but to his disappointment the local church wouldn't let him perform on their premises because of his mother's reputation. Frank felt terrible. So did his mother. She bought him a public-address system and some sheet music and he found that he could come to an agreement with local bands—he would let them have his arrangements, and they would let him sing with them. His singing was not good—some went as far as to describe it as "terrible," but Frank was extremely pushy and they couldn't say no.

By 1935 Frank had met a local trio called The Three Flashes and they allowed him to hang out with them because he had a car and they didn't. But they wouldn't let him sing. When the trio was asked to sing in a couple of short films, Frank begged them to let him join the band.

They wouldn't. With Frank in tears, Dolly got on the phone. That same afternoon Frank was made lead singer.

The films took seven days to make and Frank was paid $10 a day to wear a top hat and mime a song. They were shown at a screening at Radio City Music Hall, New York, in October 1935 and were surprisingly well received. The owner of Radio City asked the boys if they would like to be in his weekly talent contest and, on the big night, the clapometer registered highest for The Hoboken Four, as they now called themselves They were signed up at $50 a week and included in a nationwide tour with sixteen other variety acts, playing in supermarkets and parking lots. Frank became homesick. He wrote to his mother, "There's no place like Hoboken," and Dolly immediately called the *Jersey Observer* and had this printed in the society page.

Frank with his first wife, Nancy

"RUSTIC CABIN" YEARS

Frank was the only member of the group to take the tour seriously, which paid dividends—every time he crooned in a solo, women in the audience began to swoon. The other band members grew jealous, and would often tease him and beat him up. By the end of the year Frank couldn't stand it any more and he returned to Hoboken.

Back in Hoboken, Frank sang at Italian weddings, and at social clubs for $2 a night, and haunted music stations, begging them to give him work. Eventually he auditioned for a small roadside club, the Rustic Cabin, whose shows were broadcast once a week on a live link-up to a New York radio station. Frank failed the audition and went home in tears. Once again Dolly got on the phone.

Frank's new salary was $15 a week and for all his arrogant hogging of the microphone and talk about what a massive star he would soon be, no one thought he could sing. At about this time he started dating a woman called Toni Francke. Dolly was furious. On vacation with his aunt the summer before, Frank had met an Italian girl named Nancy Barbato. Nancy's family lived in Jersey City in a wooden house with a porch, which Dolly considered very respectable. Nancy, she thought, was a highly suitable match for Frank. As well as being well off, Nancy was quiet and devout, and Dolly would still be boss. Every time Toni came around,

Dolly screamed at her, calling her "cheap trash" and throwing things at her. Soon Toni became pregnant and although she had a miscarriage, Frank insisted that he'd marry her. Dolly decided that it was about time Frank married Nancy Barbato.

When Toni went down to the Rustic Cabin one day, she found Nancy in the front row, claiming to be Frank's girlfriend. A fight ensued. Toni stormed home only to reappear very shortly with two policemen and a warrant for Frank's arrest. He was charged with bringing a single female into disrepute under promise of marriage, and taken to the police cells. Toni found him there a little later, sitting on the floor and sobbing his heart out and she agreed to drop the charges if only Dolly would agree to apologize for destroying their relationship.

Dolly agreed to but never did apologize, and when Frank got home she ordered him to marry Nancy immediately. The wedding was set for February 4, 1939. Frank was wretched and none of his friends were invited. It was a miserable affair. The couple moved into an apartment in Jersey City and Nancy got a job as a secretary at $25 a week, the same amount as Frank. Frank rarely appeared in the house and spent most of their money on luxury items for himself.

In June 1939 a trumpeter named Harry James, who had recently left Benny Goodman's band to start his own, heard Frank on the radio and turned up at the Rustic Cabin to have a look. Frank had evidently improved since the early days because Harry immediately offered Frank a contract at $75 a week. Frank made his first appearance with Harry James and His Music Makers at the Hippodrome in Baltimore within a few weeks, singing popular favorites like "On a Little Street in Singapore."

Album cover to Sinatra's record Come Fly with Me

Recording with Count Basie

FAME AT LAST

That Christmas, in Chicago, the band had second billing to the Tommy Dorsey Orchestra, who were very big at the time. The lead singer of the Tommy Dorsey Orchestra casually mentioned to his band leader that he might leave and Dorsey, a hugely temperamental man, saw this as an insult and immediately offered Frank the singer's job instead. Harry James did not hold Frank to his contract and as soon as he had prepared his replacement singer, Frank left to join the Tommy Dorsey Orchestra.

Within a few months Frank had recorded "I'll Never Smile Again," which went straight to number one and stayed there for weeks. Tommy began putting Frank's name above everyone else's on the billing, and Buddy Rich, their star drummer, in particular resented him and would alter the tempo while Frank was singing. Once Frank threw a heavy glass jug at his head; on another occasion Buddy attacked Frank with his cymbals; both could have been seriously injured. Yet some years later Frank was to give Buddy, who was setting up his own band, $40,000. The other band members all found him excessively arrogant, but Tommy recognized his talent, and Frank adored Tommy. When Nancy had a daughter, Little Nancy, on June 7, 1940, he made the bandleader her godfather. In all this time, however, Frank never actually appeared at home and made no pretense about his many affairs, complaining openly about his dull and nagging wife.

In October 1940 the band went to Hollywood to appear in their first feature film as the onstage band. By the second day Frank had met a blonde starlet named Alora Gooding, and within a week she had moved into his hotel room. She was just the first of many. In May 1941 Frank, age twenty-five, was voted top band vocalist in *Billboard* magazine, and by the end of the year he had displaced Bing Crosby as "most popular singer." Frank, now more arrogant than ever, was determined to have a solo recording career under his own name. Tommy could do little to stop him and so, though he was now making $13,000 a year and everyone in the band thought he was crazy, Frank left the band and found himself an agent and a recording contract. The gamble paid off. The agency MCA offered Tommy $60,000 ($25,000 from Sinatra) to buy out Frank's contract, and he was soon making records. But Frank never forgave Dorsey for not letting him out of his contract without putting up a fight.

In December 1942 Benny Goodman, the King of Swing, was booked to appear in a show at New York's Paramount Theatre. The main singer was Peggy Lee and the manager decided to add Frank as support. The second he stepped on stage, the girls went mad. A press agent named George Evans was at that show. The next morning he went to see Frank.

George Evans already represented Duke Ellington, Lena Horne, Dean Martin, and others of their caliber, and was determined to make his new client the most sensational singer in the country. The next day he hired twelve girls at a rate of five dollars each and he rehearsed them furiously. He distributed hundreds of free tickets to local schoolchildren so that the theater was packed and then he invited the press to that evening's show to witness the new phenomenon. They arrived to see scores of hysterical girls moaning, fainting, and throwing themselves onto the stage. It was pandemonium. The next day's papers were full of the story. Although only twelve girls had been hired, thirty had fainted, and that evening lines began to form around the block. The theater remained sold out for eight weeks and George Evans started up 250 Sinatra fan clubs around the country, constantly feeding the press stories about the insane devotion of Frank's fans.

George created a whole new biography for his client, making him twenty-six rather than twenty-eight and elevating him from high school dropout to college graduate. He said that Frank had been a sports reporter on the *Jersey Observer* and that both of Frank's parents were born in America and his mother was a Red Cross nurse. He told Nancy to have her teeth capped and her nose altered by plastic surgery and he took her to buy new clothes. Within a few weeks Frank returned to the Paramount and security men had to be hired to stop the girls from swamping the stage. The New York City Education Department threatened to press charges for encouraging truancy in teenage girls.

Frank's entourage now boasted a large number of burly Italian men, including two bodyguards. Every Friday night Frank took them to Madison Square Garden to watch the boxing; here Frank would see his neighbor, Willie Moretti, the underworld boss of New Jersey, who introduced him to other mobsters. Frank and his followers loved the whole scene and imitated the mannerisms of the low-life crooks, thinking that they were manly and tough.

Soon Frank was offered his first real film role, a starring part in *Higher and Higher.* In August 1943 everyone in his entourage except the Nancys (Big Nancy was pregnant) set off for Hollywood, where George had booked him in to the Hollywood Bowl to sing with the Los Angeles Symphony Orchestra. It was the first time a popular singer had ever been offered this accolade and, though classical music lovers were outraged, the place was packed and it was the largest house of the season. By the end of 1943 Frank was the most popular singer in America; while psychologists explained this by saying that it was mass hysteria induced by the pressures of war, sociologists claimed that it was related to the aspirations of his mainly lower-class fans, who saw Frank as the epitome of the American Dream.

Whatever the reason, Frank was not present when Big Nancy gave birth to their son, Frank Jr., on January 10, 1944. He was in Hollywood filming *Step Lively* and starring in a radio show sponsored by Vimms Vitamins. Frank stayed on in Hollywood for almost three months after the birth and he returned to New Jersey for just a few weeks in March to tell Nancy that he now wanted to live in California, where he had bought Mary Astor's estate. Nancy was delighted to get away from Dolly, who was enjoying the reflected glory to the full, and she moved out west, taking her five married sisters with her. The change, however, did nothing to improve her marriage and she saw Frank even less than she had done before.

On September 28, 1944, Frank Sinatra was one of the guests at tea at the White House. President Roosevelt was not popular among Italian Americans and the invitation secured him the support of Sinatra, who campaigned energetically for him. Frank's fans were delighted but the press was not so sure. To many older Americans, Frank was simply a draft dodger who had become extremely rich at home while their loved ones were dying abroad. This accusation was to haunt Frank for many years. Though no one questioned Frank's popularity as a singer, all sorts of negative reports began to appear in the press about Frank the man. In 1943 a medical examination had disqualified Frank from military service on account of his punctured eardrum, but in 1945 he was called for another medical; this time he was excused from military service under a clause that exempted all "outstanding athletes and stage and screen stars" as essential to the nation. Mothers all over the country wrote in to newspapers demanding to know why Frank's crooning was considered more essential than their sons' lives. George Evans knew he had to do something and so, just days after peace was declared, he organized a concert tour of Europe, ostensibly to entertain the troops.

Frank's whole gang flew to Rome, where he insisted on their staying at the best hotels and on meeting the pope, who had never heard of him. When Frank was finally introduced to the troops there was a lot of initial ill feeling: they felt he'd been stealing their wives' hearts while they were stuck abroad. Frank played himself up as a victim—a skinny little runt who couldn't stand up for himself—and immediately endeared himself to the men. Though the press was still suspicious (it was the shortest overseas tour any of the celebrities had made to support the troops) some ground was gained.

Frank returned to the United States, where he immediately caused offense by criticizing the administration of troop entertainment. To save the situation, George Evans quickly built up Frank's persona of one campaigning against racial injustice, religious intolerance, and racial discrimination. Frank was persuaded to make a ten-minute film called *The House I Live In* (1946), which showed him teaching religious and racial tolerance to a bunch of street urchins. It was a public-relations triumph and Frank went on to give talks on tolerance, soon receiving the first scroll ever presented by the Bureau of Intercultural Education, which was handed to him by Eleanor Roosevelt herself.

Next to Eleanor's husband, however, the man whom Frank most admired was Benjamin "Bugsy" Siegel, the West Coast Mafia boss. Handsome and charming, he described himself as a "businessman" but everyone knew he had been indicted for a number of offenses, including murder and extortion. Frank would constantly boast about being Bugsy's friend and talk about how many men Bugsy had killed and how he had disposed of the bodies. Although Frank was fairly successful by this time, he was genuinely awestruck by the gangland boss and saw him as often as possible, kowtowing to his every need.

In 1946 Frank moved to MGM on a five-year contract at $260,000 a year. By this stage his records sold ten million copies a year. In January 1947 Joe Fischetti, a sworn mafioso and cousin of Al Capone, came to visit Frank. He invited the singer to visit the Mafia bosses at their annual convention in Miami before flying on to Havana where their leader, Lucky Luciano, was living in exile. It was the most exciting thing that had ever happened to Frank. He bought some guns and flew straight to Miami, where he put on a free show for "the boys" and then went on to Havana, where he met the Mafia leaders from across America.

George Evans was worried and announced that Frank was soon to appear in a film *(The Miracle of the Bells*, 1949) as a priest and that he would be donating his entire $100,000 salary to the church. Journalists were highly suspicious. Lee Mortimer, the entertainment editor of the *New York Daily*, was one of the few who dared to express his suspicions in print in a review of the film *It Happened in Brooklyn* (1948). Not long after, Frank "happened" to encounter Lee Mortimer at a nightclub. When Lee and his companion got up to leave, Frank and his three stooges followed him out of the club, pinned him to the ground, and slugged him several times. Although Frank claimed that Mortimer had started the incident, MGM attorneys encouraged him to settle the matter, and after some negative press matters were smoothed over, even if the incident did not do Frank's reputation any good.

Since Frank's only successful film to date had been *Anchors Aweigh* (1945) with Gene Kelly, MGM decided to put him back into a sailor suit. The two new films were *Take Me Out to the Ball Game* (1948) and *On the Town* (1949). Frank, who was now thirty-four, adored Gene Kelly and was very sensitive about his own inferior dancing skills and his receding hairline. He also had to have his large ears taped back for every shot and his childhood operation scars covered over with make-up. To add to these indignities, the costume designer discovered that none of the sailor suits fit Frank properly and the seat of his trousers had to be artificially padded.

Sinatra and Gene Kelley in Anchors Aweigh

Frank and Ava Gardner, 1948

AVA GARDNER YEARS

By 1948 Frank rarely saw his wife, though they did have a second daughter, Christina, born in June of that year. There was no shortage of glamorous women for Frank, but his greatest hope was to be seen as "classy" and his greatest aspiration was to capture the heart of the "classy" star Ava Gardner. So far the few times they had met had left Ava unimpressed. Then one evening they got drunk together and Frank drove her out to the desert, taking his guns along for the ride. They drove through a little desert town, shooting at shop windows, streetlamps, and even hitting a man, though fortunately he received nothing worse than a graze. The pair was arrested and locked up in the local cells. George Evans's partner, Jack Keller, received a telephone call from Frank in the middle of the night, demanding assistance.

Jack arrived within hours and, while Frank and Ava slept in the cells, he sorted out the whole matter. The arresting officers were given $2000 each; $1000 was needed to destroy the hospital records of the injured man; $2000 went to repairing damaged city property; and $5000 was given to the chief police officer who organized the deal. The shop owners got a $1000 each, and the man who had been injured got $10,000. Ava and Frank were then put on the first plane back home and Jack told Frank in no uncertain terms that he had to stop seeing Ava immediately. Frank was not a man to take orders lightly (or at all). He called George, demanding that Jack Keller be fired. Though Frank was still his biggest client, George Evans still had moral scruples and refused to be dictated to by Frank. He, too, advised Frank to stop seeing Ava. After eight years of loyal service, Frank promptly fired the man who had made him a star.

Ava Gardner was born in 1922 in North Carolina, the daughter of an tobacco farmer. Even as a child she was stunningly beautiful. At the age of eighteen she went to New York to visit her sister, who was married to a photographer. He took some pictures of her that ended up in the hands of Louis B. Mayer, the head of MGM, who sent for her to come to Hollywood. "She can't act," he said, "she can't talk, but she's a terrific piece of merchandise." She was signed up for seven years and immediately sent to work with a voice coach since her Southern accent was difficult to understand.

By the time she met Frank Sinatra, she was a different woman. She had already been married twice—first to Mickey Rooney (1942) and then to Artie Shaw (1945)—and in some ways she and Frank were perfectly suited. They were both lean and lithe, both uneducated, and both drank a lot. Without George Evans around, there was nobody able to hold Frank back from a tempestuous affair with Ava.

In 1949, however, there were no Sinatra discs among the best-selling records and people were beginning to think that the dog might have had his day. His films weren't doing too well and his teen fans had all grown up. Instead of revitalizing his career, Frank squandered all his energies on Ava, and in December 1949 he defied all social conventions by taking Ava with him to New York, where he wanted her to meet his mother. A few days later, after a short conversation with Nancy in which she refused to agree to a divorce, he walked out on his wife for good.

The publicity was horrendous. Frank was depicted as a total cad and Ava was labeled a home wrecker. Frank told the papers that his marriage was over a long time before he ever started seeing Ava but nothing could help his negative image. Still loyal to Frank, George Evans argued fiercely in his defense with a journalist and then suffered a fatal heart attack. On April 27, 1950, MGM's publicity department issued a statement announcing Sinatra's departure from the studio. It was a dismissal that had been brewing for some time and because of the number of enemies he had made over the years, no one now offered him a new contract. Ava had left to make a film in Spain and he could not promise her a wedding since Nancy refused to divorce him. Ava got fed up with waiting and began a very public affair with her costar, a Spanish bullfighter. Back in New York, Frank's voice began to falter, and on the sixth night of his new concert series, he opened his mouth and no sound came out of his throat. He had been struck down with hysterical aphonia and his vocal chords refused to work. His concerts were canceled and his life was in ruins. Frank flew straight to Spain, where the bullfighter had already told the press that he and Ava were madly in love. Frank said it was a lie but flew straight back to California. He was besotted with Ava, and for once in his life he wasn't getting his own way.

Although she would not divorce him, Nancy did hire a lawyer who negotiated a financial agreement with Frank that was most advantageous to her but crippling to her husband. He was actually obliged to borrow money since he was no longer getting a salary from MGM, his popularity was waning, and he still couldn't sing. He had made so many enemies that none of the sound editors would help him to engineer his voice, and, though he managed to get a booking for his very first television show, his temperamental behavior made him impossible to work with and the show was canceled. Unable to find other work, Frank turned to his friends in the Mafia, who got him work at a few night clubs.

In 1950 Democratic senator Estes Kefauver became the chairman of a special government committee looking into the workings of organized crime. In his possession were reams of photos of Frank Sinatra with Lucky Luciano, who was now running an international drug cartel from Cuba. Frank's presence was requested at the hearings. Frank's lawyer, knowing that a public appearance would finish his career completely, only agreed for his client to testify in strictest secrecy. Though he could not deny that he knew these men, Frank said that he knew nothing about their business interests. He escaped being charged, but the case was kept open.

Frank did at least manage to land the lead in the film *Meet Danny Wilson;* the screenplay was written by a friend of his and the storyline closely resembled Sinatra's own rise to the top. The movie was released (to no acclaim) by Universal in 1951. Frank had to promise the $25,000 fee to Nancy, and the filming was marred by further emotional outbursts from him, for Ava was now refusing to see him until he was divorced. As soon as he could, Frank hurried to Nevada to take advantage of that state's simplified divorce laws, but Nancy filed papers objecting and refused to agree unless he paid her $65,000 immediately. By October Frank was so desperate to see Ava that he conceded to every one of Nancy's demands. On October 31, 1951, Nancy was granted a divorce in Santa Monica on grounds of Frank's mental cruelty.

The date for Frank and Ava's wedding was set, then called off after a quarrel, and finally took place on November 7 in Philadelphia. When they got to the registry office, they were surrounded by reporters. As the magistrate pronounced them husband and wife, Frank announced to the guests, "We finally made it. We finally made it," and Ava ran across the room and threw her arms around her new mother-in-law. Dolly was delighted. "She's brought my Frankie back to me," she was quoted as saying. The two women got on famously; they were both fiercely committed Democrats, and they both thought that Frank was the best singer in the world. Dolly blessed the marriage and knew that Ava would do her best to kickstart Frank's lagging career.

During his twelve years with Nancy, however, Frank had always been in control of events. But Ava was a very different story. She was wild and independent and she was currently earning a lot more than Frank Sinatra. Having to pay Nancy $150,000 a year made him financially dependent on his new wife, and Frank, who had no work of his own, spent his time chasing around after her and carrying her bags. His agency fired him and even his record company, Columbia, refused to renew his contract. Ava's career, meanwhile, was soaring sky-high. MGM offered her a new contract at $100,000 a picture, and she went to Africa to film *The Snows of Kilimanjaro* for Twentieth Century-Fox. Frank meanwhile was reduced to playing a concert at a small club back in Hoboken, where he was pelted with vegetables and booed off the stage.

Frank in performance, 1950

FROM HERE TO ETERNITY

It came to Frank's attention that a new film called *From Here to Eternity* was currently being cast by Harry Cohn, the head of Columbia Pictures. Frank read the script and knew that the part of Maggio was the role he'd been destined to play his whole life. He called Harry Cohn over and over but Harry wouldn't speak to the washed-up star. Before Ava left for Africa to film *Mogambo* for MGM, she went on a secret visit to see Joan Cohn, Harry's wife, and begged her to intervene on Frank's behalf. Mrs. Cohn was stunned. It was a quite extraordinary course of action and she was touched by Ava's devotion to one she saw as a has-been. She said she would try to help.

Fueled by desperation, Frank managed to arrange a meeting with Cohn. Cohn pointed out that the part was a real acting part and Frank was not an actor, but Frank begged and made such wild promises that Cohn left him with a "we'll see." Frank then sent his agents to see director Fred Zinnemann (who said much the same thing as Cohn) and himself spoke to the producer of *From Here to Eternity*, and to a few friends. Eventually, assaulted on all sides, Cohn agreed that Sinatra might be given a screen test sometime.

The Sinatras soon left for Nairobi, celebrating their first wedding anniversary on the way. Frank gave Ava a marvelous diamond ring without telling her that he had charged it to her own credit card. "It was quite an occasion for me," she said. "I had been married twice before but never for a whole year." Just five days later, Frank received a cable saying that he could now do the screen test for *Eternity* and, despite Ava being ill and unhappy, he flew straight back to Hollywood.

Everyone was surprised to see him in the studio so soon after he'd received the telegram. He didn't need the script (he'd already learned every word of the text by heart) and, though he was better than expected, he wasn't by any means brilliant. Harry Cohn wanted Eli Wallach to play the part. Eli's screen test was in a different league from Frank's but Eli wanted a lot of money, and he had been offered a stage part for which he was ready to pull out of the film. Frank was now offering to do the part for nothing. Ava called Harry from Africa and said that if Frank didn't get the part, he would kill himself. Harry didn't know what to do. He chewed his nails and then asked his wife to watch the two tests to see what she thought. Joan agreed that Eli was a better actor but, she said, he looked too healthy. Remembering Ava, she pointed out that Frank was skinny and pathetic-looking—the right man for the job. Frank got the part.

Back in Africa, Ava had received her credit card bills. She was furious. But Frank was oblivious to the trouble besetting his tempestuous marriage. He was working with Montgomery Clift, Burt Lancaster, and Deborah Kerr, and he was a model of good behavior. He gave press interviews and he was humble and polite. He rehearsed with Clift constantly, and since neither man could stand to be alone, they drank together all night and Burt Lancaster often had to put them to bed in the early hours of the morning. *From Here to Eternity* was the biggest money-spinner in Columbia's history, all five leading players were nominated for Oscars, and, surprisingly, the best reviews came for Frank, who immediately proclaimed his comeback. He was convinced that both his career and his marriage would be salvaged but Ava wasn't so sure.

"When he was down and out, he was so sweet," she said, "but now he's back on top again, it's hell. He's become his old arrogant self." He started drinking with his old Mafia friends and expected Ava to answer to his beck and call. She would not. He, in turn, wouldn't go to the opening of *Mogambo* unless she called him personally. The situation was stalemated, and on October 29, 1953, MGM announced that their marriage was over. Frank was devastated. Alone in New York, Frank halfheartedly slit his wrists; his agents announced that he was "physically exhausted."

Suddenly Frank could sing again and the heartbreak he felt over Ava meant that he now expressed himself with more emotion than he had ever done before. He poured his heart out into ballad after ballad and created a whole new audience of broken-hearted men who all identified with his feelings of loss and betrayal. A nonproductive one-year contract with Capitol was renewed and Nelson Riddle became his musical arranger. The combination soon paid off. The partnership lasted eight years, and during this period Frank made what are considered to be his best recordings, including "Come Fly with Me," "Young at Heart" and the LP *Songs for Swingin' Lovers.*

Frank brooded over Ava. He called her constantly in Rome and in Madrid and he visited her, but she wouldn't change her mind. He spent his evenings at nightclubs and playing cards, and got drunk and maudlin. When he took women out he would bore them by talking about his wife and telling them that she was the most beautiful woman on earth. On March 25, 1954, Frank took Little Nancy (now thirteen) and Frank Jr. (now ten) to the Oscar ceremony, where he received the Best Supporting Actor award for *From Here to Eternity*. It was the biggest night of his life, but after returning the children to their mother, he spent the rest of it alone.

With President Kennedy, 1961

JFK YEARS

At this time Las Vegas was the only place in the United States where gambling was legal. Frank bought a share in one of its larger casinos, the Sands Hotel. The management wanted him in so that he would attract customers by performing; though he frequently spent all of his money at the gambling tables, this was his most favorite investment. He had a permanent suite in the hotel with a private swimming pool whcre he regularly held wild parties. Frank loved Las Vegas.

In 1954 Sinatra was again rated most popular male vocalist in a poll, and named Singer of the Year. And during that year and 1955 he made more movies than any other Hollywood star, including *Guys and Dolls*, *The Tender Trap*, and *The Pride and the Passion* with Cary Grant and Sophia Loren. By 1956 he was friends with many film folk; in particular he idolized Humphrey Bogart, who was everything Frank aspired to be—educated, sophisticated, and respected. Shortly after they became close, however, Bogart was diagnosed with throat cancer. Frank became a constant visitor to the house and got to know Bogart's wife, Lauren Bacall, particularly well. On January 14, 1957, Bogart died, and for the rest of that year, Frank and Lauren were seen together constantly. She clearly wanted to marry him; he finally proposed on March 11, 1958, but left the next day for Miami. That evening Lauren was questioned by a journalist, who put the news in the next morning's

With daughter Nancy

paper. When she finally got him on the telephone, Frank reproached her bitterly and she did not hear from him again for years. According to Ava Gardner he said that he had never had any intention of marrying "that pushy female."

Frank was gradually being accepted as a grand man of the film world and he received $3 million for a three-year contract with ABC television—one of the hottest deals ever. Although the ratings were low and the series was dropped, Frank didn't seem to care. All he really wanted was to be in the movies. In 1958, having made some ten films in the previous two years, he was rated the biggest money-making film star of the year. But he was disappointed that same year not to win the Grammy for best male vocal—and horrified when Elvis Presley appeared on the scene. In September 1959 Frank was master of ceremonies at a Twentieth Century-Fox luncheon in honor of President Khrushchev and his wife, at which four hundred of Hollywood's most glamorous people appeared. Frank turned on his full charm and good humor, sitting next to Mrs. Khrushchev and discussing her grandchildren and his children.

In 1959 Frank's life was transformed by his friendship with Peter Lawford, whose brother-in-law, John F. Kennedy, was about to run for president. The politician was brilliant, rich, and handsome, and everyone adored him. He, in turn, enjoyed touring around Hollywood with Sinatra. Frank was dazzled by JFK and threw himself into the presidential campaign with total dedication, briefly interrupting his political activities for Little Nancy's wedding in September 1960 to teenage-idol singer Tommy Sands. She was his favorite child, upon whom he had lavished the most extravagant gifts, including, for her seventeenth birthday, the first pink Thunderbird in the country.

On Election Day, November 8, 1960, the voting was so close that JFK won by a mere 18,000 votes in a total of over 68 million. Frank was beside himself with excitement and was convinced that his Palm Springs house would become the president's retreat on the West Coast. In January 1961 he flew to Washington, D.C., with Peter Lawford to organize the inauguration gala of the new president. It was the most exciting day of Frank's life. He spent $90,000 of his money for commemorative silver cigarette boxes that were distributed to every table. For the next three hours the stadium was filled with the glitterati of the entertainment world, including Ella Fitzgerald, Laurence Olivier and Gene Kelly. At the end JFK himself came on stage and thanked everyone involved, particularly Frank Sinatra. Frank was in heaven. He paid to have the president's entire speech reprinted in *Variety* and then had a recording made, which he played over and over to his friends.

Returning home to L.A. was an anticlimax and Frank sat around his pool with a gang of friends, including Marilyn Monroe and Sammy Davis Jr. Though JFK was very grateful to Sinatra, the president didn't invite the performer to the White House. It soon became clear that the invitation would never happen, when JFK appointed his brother, Bobby, to the post of attorney general and encouraged him to set up a new task force against organized crime. Included in the initial list of top suspects were most of Frank's closest friends. Both JFK and Bobby agreed that, under no circumstances, could the president ever stay at the home of a man who had also played host to known Mafia bosses. Frank couldn't believe it. He'd had a whole presidential wing specially constructed on his estate. He had to blame someone and he chose the unfortunate Peter Lawford as a scapegoat. Lawford was immediately cut out of all Frank's films and his career never recovered.

Frank was filming when he heard the news of JFK's assassination, which devastated him. However, to his deep disappointment, he was not invited to JFK's funeral—the company he was known to keep made him too much of an embarrassment to the Kennedys. Then, just a few weeks later, Frank's son was kidnapped at gunpoint. It was the biggest kidnapping in America for years and scared Sinatra badly. Ultimately all went well: Bobby Kennedy immediately had the FBI on the case, Frank paid the ransom, Frank Jr. was released, and the kidnappers were arrested the next day.

an awards ceremony with Grace Kelly, Gregory Peck, and Barbara Marx

Frank with Mia Farrow

MIA FARROW

In 1964 Frank began filming *Von Ryan's Express.* Toward the end of the shoot a nineteen-year-old girl with long golden hair appeared on the set. Her name was Mia Farrow. She was a true child of Hollywood, born in 1945 to actress Maureen O'Sullivan and director John Farrow. She was in New York playing the heroine in *Peyton Place,* a popular television show, and she had set her heart on meeting Frank Sinatra. Every day she turned up and hung around the set. After a few weeks she heard Frank talking about going to the desert for the weekend and she ran over and said, "How come you never invite me to come along?" Frank, now almost fifty, immediately invited her to join the group and the two became an item.

He called her constantly on the set of *Peyton Place* and the couple told the press that they were in love. Though she was younger than two of Frank's children, the pair skipped about like young colts, and on July 4 he gave Mia an engagement ring. After one of his friends told him that he was too old to marry Mia, he arranged the wedding for the very next day—they married on July 19, 1966. No members of Frank's family attended, though Dolly later organized a small party at her house. She wasn't impressed. Mia, she said, didn't eat, didn't talk, and had never been in a film. It couldn't last.

When comedian Jackie Mason began a routine making fun of Frank's marriage to Mia, he soon began to receive death threats. He didn't change his act, and a few days later an armed assailant climbed onto his patio and fired three bullets through the window. Some days later a man grabbed him from his car and smashed his face. Other similar incidents occurred whenever anyone tried to criticize Frank. No one pressed charges.

In 1967 Mia was signed up for *Rosemary's Baby.* She also managed to get herself the lead role in a television remake of the film *Johnny Belinda.* Frank couldn't bear the competition and thought that being in films was more important to Mia than her marriage. He did, however, want her to work with him in his next film, *The Detective.* She turned up on the set of *Johnny Belinda* badly bruised and battered, but still wanted to go on. Further dissent in the marriage was highlighted by their disagreements over the war in Vietnam—Mia could not understand Frank's support for the use of napalm and Agent Orange. He got drunk and went to boxing matches. She got stoned, ate yogurt, and meditated. Frank couldn't stand it any more. He told her to stop work immediately on *Rosemary's Baby* in order to start on *The Detective* but Mia just carried on. Frank filed for divorce without even speaking to his wife. Mia was devastated but she agreed to a quick divorce, refusing the generous alimony Frank offered: she didn't want money, she said, she just wanted Frank's continued friendship.

Von Ryan's Express

Frank and Barbara

LATER YEARS

In 1969 Marty Sinatra died, and after much persuasion from Frank, Dolly eventually agreed to move to Palm Springs, where her son built her a fine, large house. That same year saw the release of the album *My Way*, the title song having become Frank's signature tune. Also in that year, Mario Puzo's novel *The Godfather* was published; it caused Sinatra considerable annoyance because he felt that the character of Johnny Fontane was based on himself—connections with the Mafia were a sore point. He argued against a subpoena to appear before a New Jersey commission on organized crime, but agreed at last to a secret session in February 1970. There he denied all knowledge of his friends' Mafia connections and was again not charged. It was not the last time this was to happen.

In March 1971, after a year of poor record sales and miserable reviews, Frank announced his retirement. He had made fifty-five films, over a hundred albums, and two thousand recordings. To the astonishment of many people, he suddenly switched his lifetime political allegiance and became involved in the right-wing Republican cause, which he had previously detested.

Frank began seeing Barbara, the wife of Zeppo Marx, second-youngest of the five brothers. After divorcing Zeppo in 1973, Barbara devoted herself to Frank, to whom she was apparently perfectly suited (except in Dolly's eyes)—she was pretty, cheerful, did whatever he wanted, and never contradicted him. They finally got married in July 1976, when he was sixty and the bride a respectable forty-six. Before that, however, Frank started singing again, marking his 1974 comeback with a concert tour of the United States, followed by an international tour. Barbara accompanied him everywhere.

In January 1977 Dolly was killed in a plane crash and Frank was beside himself with grief. He turned to the Catholic Church for solace and decided that he wanted to remarry his wife before a Catholic priest. Barbara, a Protestant, obligingly converted to his religion. She also began to do serious charity work and to join all of the establishment wives' committees. Frank had received several awards for humanitarian acts, having become well known for his spontaneous generosity toward often complete strangers who were in some sort of trouble. The world began to hail the couple as generous sponsors of good causes. When Ronald Reagan took office in 1981, Frank was once again asked to chair an inaugural gala. Though he hadn't actually been invited to stand on the steps of the White House during the ceremony, he did so anyway and no one dared stop him.

For nearly twenty years Sinatra's gaming license had been under scrutiny for his violation of Nevada's gaming regulations by allowing certain undesirable characters to frequent his casinos. Eventually, in 1981, the Nevada Gaming Board gathered to hear the evidence against Sinatra. Large numbers of key establishment figures and stars testified to his philanthropy and generosity—the state of Nevada had benefited greatly from his actions. Frank denied ever having met most of his best friends. The board renewed Frank's license for six months; the Nevada Gaming Control Commission, by a vote of four to one, made the renewal indefinite.

Apart from the occasional cameo role Frank no longer made films, but he did release a number of new records, all of which sold incredibly well. He was paid $2 million for four concerts in Argentina and he also performed at the notorious

Sun City resort in Bophuthatswana, South Africa. The United Nations Special Committee against Apartheid placed him at the top of a list of entertainers who should be blacklisted for supporting apartheid but, by this time, he was untouchable. Nancy Reagan invited him to solo luncheons constantly and she asked him to organize the concert for Queen Elizabeth's visit in 1983, which was generally considered to be a complete disaster.

In 1984 Frank was put in charge of fund-raising for the presidential reelection campaign and he did such a fine job that, in 1985, President Reagan awarded him America's highest civilian award, the Presidential Medal of Freedom. In 1986, at the age of seventy-one, he became the oldest person ever to have a hit record in Britain with his recording of the song "New York, New York," and in 1993 he released a high-tech new album called *Duets*, on which he sang with such stars as Luther Vandross and Chrissie Hynde. Since he was now somewhat less mobile than in former days, the guest artists added their vocals to tapes already preprepared by Frank. Some singers attended studios while others simply phoned their contributions down digital phone lines. Everyone who was anyone apparently wanted to cut a disc with Frank, even if they weren't to be accorded the honor of actually meeting the star. The record was his biggest success in years and one song in particular, which he recorded with Bono from U2, sold five million copies.

Following the popularity of *Duets*, Frank recorded *Duets II* and in 1994 he went to Radio City Music Hall to accept a Grammy award for a lifetime of achievement in the recording industry. Four days later, while singing "My Way" in Richmond, Virginia, he collapsed on stage, but by June 1995 he was back on his feet at the grand opening of the new Beverly Hills Hotel, alongside Liza Minnelli and Sir Anthony Hopkins. The small boy from Hoboken who hung out with hoodlums had made it to the very top, where he intended to remain—rich, retired, respected, and revered. Dolly would be proud of him.

Frank with Nancy Reagan

INDEX

INDEX